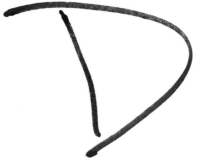

ANIMALS IN U.S. HISTORY

BISON

Lynn M. Stone

Rourke
Publishing LLC
Vero Beach, Florida 32964

www.rourkepublishing.com

PHOTO CREDITS:
Cover, title page, pp. 4, 6, 7, 8, 20, 22 © Lynn M. Stone; pp. 12, 13 © James P. Rowan; pp. 14, 16, 18, 19 courtesy of The Kansas State Historical Society, Topeka; p. 10 courtesy of Library of Congress

Title page: *Bison still roam a few western prairies in dawn light.*

Editor: Frank Sloan

Cover design by Nicola Stratford
Interior design by Heather Scarborough

Library of Congress Cataloging-in-Publication Data

Stone, Lynn M.
Bison / Lynn M. Stone.
    p. cm. — (Animals in U.S. history)
Summary: Introduces the American bison and its importance in the history of Native Americans and of the United States.
Includes bibliographical references and index.
ISBN 1-58952-698-8 (hardcover)
1. American bison—History—Juvenile literature. 2. West
(U.S.)—History—Juvenile literature. [1. Bison--History. 2. Indians of
North America—Great Plains—History. 3. West (U.S.)—History.] I.
Title. II. Series: Stone, Lynn M. Animals in U.S. history.
QL737.U53S7434 2003
599.64'3'0978—dc21

                                                              2003009719

Printed in the USA

TABLE OF CONTENTS

Bison in the Old West

The American bison is one of the great **symbols** of the American West with good reason. Few animals have been as important to the history of Western North America as the bison.

Bison (sometimes called buffalo) were common in the West in the early 1800s. Experts say there were from 30 million to even 200 million of these big, shaggy cousins of cattle. They lived largely on grasslands, the wide North American **prairies**.

North American bison look something like the buffalo of Asia and Africa, but they belong to a different group of hoofed animals.

The bison helped shape the prairie and the community of prairie animals. Bison chewed up grass and their tramping feet plowed up ground. But bison didn't stay too long in one place. And as they moved on, their droppings **fertilized** the soil and grasses.

Bison lived in open woodlands and hiked into mountain meadows, but they were most common on the grasslands.

Bison moved easily from one area of grassland to another.

Millions of trampling bison hooves helped trees from taking root in the open prairie. The great, moving herds of bison actually kept the grasslands healthy!

Bison make dust baths for themselves by digging out hollows in the prairie dirt. When the hollows fill with rainwater, they become pools. Many prairie creatures drink from the pools. Some prairie insects and **amphibians** lay their eggs in them.

A bison bull wallows in a dust bath in South Dakota.

Bison and Plains Indians

In the mid-1800s, more and more white settlers headed westward into Indian country. Some pioneers followed bison trails. The railroad came, too, and some of the new tracks were laid out along bison paths.

While bison were important to nature, they were also important to people. In fact, the welfare of more than 25 Indian tribes was tied to the welfare of bison.

Plains Indians were skillful horsemen and bison hunters. They eventually traded in their spears for rifles.

The Plains Indians used nearly every part of a bison. For example, they used bison hides for moccasins, buckets, drums, saddles, and **teepees**. They used bison muscle for meat and thread. They used the bison's stomach lining for water bottles.

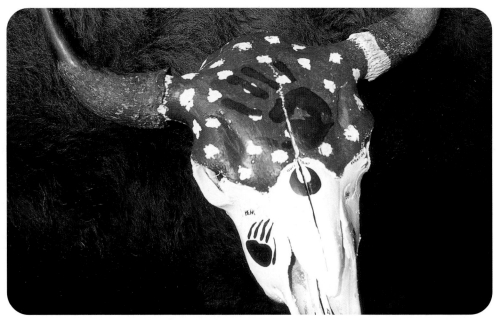

Plains Indians used almost every scrap of a bison until they began trading bison skins to white traders.

An actor at Bent's Old Fort National Historic Site in Colorado wears a bison coat like the mountain men of the 19th century.

Bison hooves were boiled into glue. Bison fat was made into soap and candles. Dry buffalo droppings, or chips, were burned for fuel.

The Changing West

The old buffalo trails led settlers and a growing nation westward. But they also led to trouble. The arrival of white settlers and railroad workers created conflict with the Indians. To weaken the Indians, the U.S. Government encouraged the killing of bison. Army soldiers, settlers, sportsmen, and railroad crews killed bison. Traders sent thousands of bison hides eastward by train.

Bison were often slaughtered by shooters who stood on the platform of railroad cars that crossed the plains. This drawing was printed in Harper's Weekly *in 1867.*

Bison had allowed the Indians to live freely in broad areas. By allowing the unlimited **slaughter** of bison, the government knew it could force Indians into farming. There was terrible waste. Many times a 2,000-pound (907-kilogram) bison bull was killed only for its tasty tongue.

The bison herd could not withstand the killing or the diseases spread by settlers' cattle. Early in 1883 hunters destroyed a herd of 10,000 bison. It was the last big hunt.

Not all bison were wasted by white hunters. Here is a pile of bison hides in Dodge City, Kansas, in 1874.

Suddenly, many *millions* of bison had become just hundreds. An animal that had shaped the prairie and the cultures of the Plains Indians was now, mostly, a pile of bones.

Killing bison in large numbers was considered "sport." This drawing first appeared in Harper's Weekly *in 1874.*

In this drawing from another 1874 Harper's, *workers cure bison hides. Bison bones in the background piles were ground into fertilizer.*

And as the government had planned, the Indians were no longer fighters or travelers.

Bison Today

In the mid-1890s, the U.S. Government agreed to protect the few remaining wild bison in Yellowstone National Park. In the early 1900s, the United States began to start bison **refuges**.

There are perhaps 300,000 bison in North America today. Only in Yellowstone and Wood Buffalo Park, however, do bison wander freely. Bison are back, but they are largely behind fences.

American bison are at home in several western refuges, including here at Theodore R. Roosevelt National Park, North Dakota.

Glossary

amphibians (am FIB ee enz) — salamanders, toads,
and frogs; cold-blooded animals with soft bodies,
moist skin, and backbones

fertilized (FERT ul EYZD) — to make healthy
for growing

prairies (PRER eez) — the native grasslands of central
North America

refuges (REF yuj ez) — fixed places of safety
for animals

slaughter (SLOT er) — killing, usually in large numbers

symbols (SIM belz) — things that stand for something,
such as a flag standing for a country

teepees (TEE PEEZ) — tall, cone-shaped dwellings
of certain American Indian tribes

*A bison bull sheds early morning frost in Yellowstone National Park.
Bison that wander out of the park are often shot.*

Index

Further Reading

Find out more about bison with these helpful books:

• Ritchie, Rita and Todd Wilkinson. *The Wonder of Bison.* Gareth Stevens, 1966.
• Robbins, Ken. *Thunder on the Plains: The Story of American Buffalo.* Atheneum, 2001.
• Winner, Cherie. *Bison.* NorthWord Press, 2001.
• Wrobel, Scott. *Bison.* Creative Education, 2000.

Websites to Visit

• www.nps.gov/wica/bison.htm
• www.pbs.org/wnet/nature/buffalo/

About the Author

Lynn Stone is a talented natural history photographer and writer. Lynn, a former teacher, travels worldwide to photograph wildlife in their natural habitat. He has more than 500 children's books to his credit.